D0571672

THE LIFE & TIMES OF
MOTHER TERESA

THE LIFE & TIMES OF

Mother
Teresa

BY
Tanya Rice

This edition first published by Parragon Books

Produced by
Magpie Books Ltd
7 Kensington Church Court
London W8 4SP

Copyright © Parragon Book Service Ltd 1994

Cover picture & illustrations courtesy of: Rex Features.

ISBN 1 85813 952 X

A copy of the British Library Cataloguing in Publication
Data is available from the British Library.

Typeset by Hewer Text Composition Services, Edinburgh
Printed in Singapore by Printlink International Co.

Mother Teresa

A small, aged woman, wrapped in a simple white sari, moves between the beds, embracing the children. Their large, dark eyes shine out of frail faces. The utter poverty that has brought these children into her care is temporarily forgotten in her presence. She replaces deprivation with her love and, in accordance with her religion, with the love of God. Few people would fail to recognise this woman. She is Mother Teresa. Her only ambition has been to alleviate the suffering of the poorest of the poor, and for this she is renowned and respected around the world.

Agnes Bojaxhiu, as Mother Teresa was christened, was born on 26 August 1910, the youngest of Nikola and Drana's three children. Lazar, her brother, was born in 1907 and her sister, Aga, in 1904, and they grew up together in Skopje, a small Serbian town. The family were, however, Albanian, living within Skopje's Albanian community. They had a pet name in their native language for their youngest member, 'Gonxha', meaning 'flower bud', because, as her brother Lazar once explained, she was pink and plump.

Agnes was born into unstable times, with 1910 seeing the first Albanian uprising. Within two years the Balkan States would be at war, and this unrest would culminate in 1914 with the outbreak of the First World War. Luckily, Agnes's father was a successful merchant and the family remained financially secure through this unsettling time. All three children attended the school which was attached to their local church. Then, when Agnes was only eight, her father suddenly died. Drana was grief-stricken for several months, but the needs of her children finally forced her to take control of the situation.

The daughter of a landowner and merchant, Drana was no stranger to hard work, and with admirable courage she quickly established her own business, selling embroidery and, later, the carpets for which Skopje was renowned. Inevitably, Drana would be one of the deepest influences on her youngest daughter. As well as being strong and re-

3

sourceful, Drana was a profoundly religious
woman who led the family's recitation of the
rosary every evening. The children called
her 'Nana Loke', meaning 'Mother of My
Soul', and grew used to welcoming strangers
at the dinner-table as Drana made a habit of
inviting the poorer members of their community to join the family at mealtimes. She
also found waste of any kind intolerable and
one evening, when the children were idly
chatting, she turned the light out, telling
them that it was a waste of electricity.

Religion played a part in almost every aspect
of Agnes's life. As members of the predomi-
nantly Albanian parish of the Sacred Heart,
her family's social life, as well as religious life,
revolved around the church which was itself
a focus for the Albanian community's cus-
toms and traditions. With her elder sister,

Aga, Agnes attended Skopje's state secondary school where she was, by all accounts, a good student, though Aga may have been the better scholar. The two girls spent a great deal of time together and shared a love of music. They both joined the church choir and the larger Albanian Catholic Choir. Agnes's brother, Lazar, on the other hand, preferred sports and spent his free time with young men of his own age. He once recalled that he had a particular weakness for sweet things and would raid the pantry at night for treats. Agnes would remind him that he should not have any food after midnight if he was to attend mass in the morning, but she never told their mother of his lapses. In 1924 Lazar left home to join a military academy in Austria, leaving Agnes's family without any man to head it in the traditional sense. In 1925, however, Father Jambrenkoic of the Society of Jesus became the local pastor and he would guide young Agnes. At the age of twelve, she had already expressed a desire to become a nun.

Father Jambrenkoic set up a branch of the Sodality of the Blessed Virgin Mary for his younger parishioners. Originally established in 1563, the Sodality drew inspiration from St Ignatius Loyola's questions: 'What have I done for Christ? What am I doing for Christ? What will I do for Christ?' Of course, Agnes joined and the group would provoke and stimulate her thoughts and feelings about God. The Sodality also focused on the lives of other saints and also of missionaries. Father Jambrenkoic was particularly enthusiastic about the missionary work of the Jesuits, and most especially about their work with the poor and with

lepers. He told stories and read letters from
Yugoslav priests who had gone to Bengal in
1924, some of whom were stationed in the
outskirts of Calcutta. Agnes caught his
enthusiasm and would help Father Jambrenkoic to describe the missionaries' work to
local people, drawing on a map to show
where the missions were at the time. Agnes
was also a member of a prayer group whose
particular concern was praying for the
church's missions in India. Their work
inspired her so much that she asked her
cousin who taught mandolin to give his
earnings to her for the missions in India.

When Drana made her regular pilgrimage to
the shrine of Our Lady of Cernagore in
Letnice, in the mountains of Montenegro,
she encouraged her daughters to accompany
her. At this time Agnes's health needed extra

7

care as she was prone to malaria and whooping cough, and therefore the mountain air was particularly good for her. Agnes loved to spend her spare time reading, but on these trips it was her sister's particular responsibility to take Agnes on long walks and then make sure that she rested. In 1928, on the feast of the Assumption, the three women made their last visit to Letnice together. Agnes had spent six years trying to understand her wish to become a nun, trying to be sure. Father Jambrenkoic had told her that if she had a vocation she would feel an intense joy, joy at the thought of serving God. Finally, Agnes was sure that she was meant to be a nun and, furthermore, a missionary. After all she had read and heard about it, her heart was set on India, and in Letnice that year she knew that the time had come for her to follow her vocation. When

Agnes told her mother, Drana stayed in her
room for twenty-four hours; one can ima-
gine how Drana struggled with herself,
neither wanting to see another member of
her family leave, nor wanting to deny the
will of God. Finally she gave Agnes her
blessing and offered her some advice: 'Put
your hand in His hand and walk all the way
with Him.' It was advice that Agnes would
never forget.

Agnes applied to the Order of Loreto Nuns,
whose work as missionaries in Bengal she
had heard so much about. She was accepted
and left Skopje on 25 September 1928. She
had to go to Zagreb first to meet up with
another noviciate, Betike Kanjc, so that they
could make the next leg of their journey
together. It was in Zagreb that Agnes said her
final goodbyes to the friends who had come

to wish her well, and to her mother and sister who had accompanied her. Agnes was only eighteen and, sad as she must have felt that day, she did not know that she would never see her mother again. The two young women had to undertake the difficult journey to Ireland and the Loreto Nuns' Mother House in Rathfarman. They were setting off for a new life and their apprehension must have been tinged with excitement.

The Loreto Order is the Irish branch of the Institute of the Blessed Virgin Mary and was founded in 1609 by Mary Ward who was, in fact, from Yorkshire. Her epitaph sums up her vocation: 'To love the poor, preserve the same, live, die and rise with them, was all the aim of Mary Ward.' Eventually, after a somewhat patchy history, the Order was asked to establish a post in Calcutta. It is easy to see what drew the young Agnes to them.

As a noviciate, Agnes spent six weeks learning English and getting her first real taste of what life would be like within the order she had chosen. She would complete her training as a noviciate in Darjeeling in India. On 6 January 1929, the Feast of Epiphany, she arrived in Calcutta, but this first visit would be brief as she still had to travel another 450 miles to reach her destination.

The British had used Darjeeling, nestling in the foothills of the Himalayas and surrounded by tea plantations, as a resting-place for their troops in the mid-nineteenth century. It quickly became a popular hill-station: a new road, a sanatorium and a hotel were built. Darjeeling boomed and by 1857

Mother Teresa of Calcutta

Entrance to the Home for the Dying

this once-secluded spot had some 10,000 inhabitants and the 1880s saw the completion of its famous mini-railway. An enclave of the British Empire, it was far removed from the filth and poverty of Calcutta. Agnes's life behind the walls of the Loreto Convent in Darjeeling settled down into a routine of prayer, teaching and receiving instructions from the novice mistress.

Nearly two and a half years after she arrived in India, Agnes took her first vows as a Sister of Loreto on 24 May 1931. She chose to be named after her patron saint, St Therese of Lisieux or St Therese of the Child Jesus. Saint Therese died young of tuberculosis, but it was her love of missions and prayers for priests, especially missionaries, which had inspired the Pope to name her, and St Francis Xavier, patron of all missions around the world. There was a complication, however, as another novice called Therese was already at the convent Agnes adopted the Spanish spelling. She was now Sister Teresa.

Having served another six years as a noviciate, Sister Teresa took her lifelong vows of poverty, chastity and obedience on 14 May 1937. She was now ready to move on from Darjeeling. She was sent to the Loreto Convent in Entally, an eastern district of Calcutta. Here, the Loreto Nuns had a large property called St Mary's where they ran a girls' school for some 500 pupils, mostly boarders who had been orphaned. In fact, the convent had originally been established as an orphanage for children of all denominations. A high wall surrounded the compound which also included a smaller school attended by local Bengali girls, most of whom were middle-class.

Far from home, Sister Teresa discovered an unexpected link to Skopje in St Mary's School. Here there was an active branch of the same organisation that had so influenced her own schoolgirl years, the Sodality of the Blessed Virgin. The members of this branch worked to relieve the terrible poverty of families living in the slum so near to the convent. Their work was guided by Father Julien Henry, the priest at St Teresa's. Every Saturday some of the girls would visit the slum while others went to the large Nilratan Sarkar Hospital with the aim of comforting the poor and the sick. Sister Teresa would encourage the girls' work, though she could not accompany them herself. Perhaps one person, her pupil Subashini Das, saw the potential that Sister Teresa had as a leader who might set an even more active example to the girls.

In order to teach at the schools, Sister Teresa had to learn Bengali, to which she would add Hindi, whilst she also became fluent in English. She taught geography and then history in both schools, and gave her full commitment to her religious life as part of the community she had joined. No one could have guessed at that time that the young Sister would one day give up this life and leave the convent. The very poor were never far from her thoughts, however, and the life of the convent was not so secluded that the Sisters never left its walls. Sister Teresa's teaching also took her to the local church's primary school, St Teresa's. This meant leaving the clean and ordered life of the convent and walking through the poverty-stricken streets of the nearby slums. Before coming to Entally, the young Sister had never seen poverty like this.

By the early 1940s India was entering a period of turmoil as Britain slowly lost its grip on its Empire. In 1943 India suffered a disastrous famine which cost at least two million lives: previously boats used to transport rice had been redeployed for the British war effort. As India found itself tragically drawn into a war it had nothing to do with, Gandhi's non-violent resistance to British rule intensified. The uncertain times brought internal unrest between the Muslim and Hindu communities. 16 August 1946 was declared 'Direct Action Day' by the Muslim League; in Calcutta, the head of the administration, who was Muslim, de-

clared it a public holiday. The tension
between Muslims and Hindus boiled over
into terrible violence and the city was
paralysed. Later, Mother Teresa would re-
call, 'I saw bodies on the streets, stabbed,
beaten, lying there in dried blood.' 1947
would bring partition and India would
finally be released from British rule, but
not without massive disruption and still
more violence. Sixteen million people were
on the move as Hindus and Sikhs fled into
India, whilst Muslims headed to Pakistan.
Calcutta would become the new home of
many displaced and desperately poor people.

It is against this background that Sister
Teresa's early life as a nun must be seen.
For, while it would have been perfectly
normal for her to stay at the convent for
the rest of her life, these were not normal

times and there was no telling what one might be called upon to do.

The only other regular excursion Sister Teresa would make outside the convent was an annual retreat to Darjeeling, where she would concentrate on deepening her religious commitment. It was on the train to Darjeeling for one such retreat that Sister Teresa experienced what she has since called 'an inner command'. It was 10 September 1946, nine and a half years after her move to Calcutta. She has described how God told her to renounce her life within the Convent and go into the slums to work and live among the poorest of the poor. 'The message was quite clear, it was an order. I was to leave the Convent. I felt that God wanted something more from me. He wanted me to be poor and to love Him in the distressing

disguise of the poorest of the poor.' She felt
the call all through her retreat and knew that
she must answer it.

When she first returned from Darjeeling, she
sought the permission she would need if she
were to follow the direction of her new
calling. She shared her thoughts with other
Sisters and sought the support of her superiors, including the Archbishop of Calcutta.
Keeping her identity secret, the Archbishop
discussed the matter with Father Henry and
with Father Celeste van Exem, Sister Teresa's spiritual director. Father van Exem was
a key figure in Sister Teresa's spiritual
development and was one of the first to
know of the 'inner command' that was
compelling her. He guided her in her dealings with the Archbishop of Calcutta and it
was he who eventually told her that permis-

Inside Nirmal Hriday

The Children's Home of the Immaculate

sion had been granted, that her prayers had
been answered. When the time came, Sister
Teresa asked him to bless a simple sari, the
kind that every poor Bengali woman wore,
and a small cross and rosary. These were the
symbols she chose for her new role.

The Archbishop could see that the Daughters of St Anne were already involved in the
sort of work Sister Teresa had been called to
do, and so he suggested that she join.
However, it was their practice to return to
the seclusion of the convent at the end of
each day's work among the poor. Sister
Teresa was clear that not only had she been
called to work with the poor, but she was
also to live among them. This complicated
matters because Sister Teresa would have to
be released from the Loreto Order as no one
within it was doing similar work. She was

told to write to the Mother General of Loreto in Dublin and ask for her permission to leave the congregation. Sister Teresa's calling would now take her down one of two paths: she had either to ask her Mother General for secularization, which would mean she would no longer be a nun; or she could ask for exclaustration, which would enable her to leave her closed order, but still be bound by her vows of poverty, chastity and obedience. If she were no longer a nun, it would be difficult, even impossible, to get others to join her and so begin a new religious community to fulfil the calling God had given her. For unknown reasons, it seems that the Archbishop told Sister Teresa that she must apply for secularization and, despite Father van Exem's intervention, insisted that she put her faith in God. When the Mother General's reply came, Sister Teresa had been granted exclaustration. One further hurdle remained: she now had to write to Rome and seek the same permission, and again the Archbishop insisted that she ask for secularization.

This final stage was neither easy nor speedy,- and to Sister Teresa – so clear that God had called her not only to work, but also to live with the poor – the wait seemed endless. On 7 August 1948 the letter from Rome, dated 12 April, finally arrived in Calcutta. Sister Teresa's prayers had been answered: she could leave the Loreto Order, but remain a nun. She would keep her vows of poverty and chastity, but, instead of being bound to the Loreto Order, she now owed her obedience to the Archbishop of Calcutta.

It was what she had wanted, what she knew God was calling her to do; yet leaving the Convent at Entally and the community which had been so much a part of her life was one of the hardest things for Sister Teresa to sacrifice. 'Loreto meant everything to me', she once said. On being given the news of Sister Teresa's mission, the other Sisters were told neither to question nor to praise her decision. She was on her own.

The first thing Sister Teresa needed was some medical training, as there would be little hope of helping the 'poorest of the poor' without it. So when she left the Loreto Order in her simple sari and sandals, she set off for Petna, a city on the Ganges some 240 miles from Calcutta. Here the Medical Mission Sisters would introduce

Sister Teresa to some basic medical skills. Sister Teresa always talked to the other Sisters about the spiritual side of her new calling, in which the time given to prayer, penance and fasting would be as important as the work she would carry out. Hearing this, there was one thing that the Sisters stressed to Sister Teresa: if she was to be of any use to the poor as God intended, then she had an obligation to look after her own health. She must not let her compassion for the poor lead her to neglect her personal hygiene or the rest she would need in order to work effectively, and she must maintain a healthy diet. She could not, they told her, eat as little as the poor and expect to keep her health. She would have to combine her spiritual life with a practical approach if she wished to be of any service to the poor.

After almost four months with the Medical Mission Sisters, Sister Teresa was granted permission to return to Calcutta where Father van Exem had found her a place with the Little Sisters of the Poor at their house for the elderly, the St Joseph's home. Here she divided her time between looking after the home's elderly residents and visiting the poor in the bustee or slum at Motijhil, the workers' housing which was just outside the Loreto Convent in Entally. She established a school at Motijhil, the bustee she had only been able to look down on from the convent's windows, simply by starting to write out the alphabet one day in the dirt. Before long, there were donations of chairs and a blackboard, and eventually she was able to hire a couple of rooms for her small school. It was hard and lonely work, and Sister Teresa sometimes felt the pull of the

The Missionaries of Charity

Calcutta street children

familiarity and comforts of her old life at the convent. At such times she turned to God to give her the courage and strength she needed to continue with the work she knew she had been called to do.

The next step was for Sister Teresa to find a place where she could develop her work independently. She approached Father van Exem who, in turn, sought the help of Michael Gomes, a Bengali Catholic who lived with his family in a large three-storey house, 14 Creek Lane. Half of the house was empty and it was Michael's young daughter Mabel who suggested that Sister Teresa use the space to begin her work.

February 1949 found Sister Teresa moving into 14 Creek Lane with just one small suitcase. For a brief period Sister Teresa

kept a journal recording her work, and the
entry she made on that first night at Creek
Lane reveals how hard it was for her to begin
with:

28 February

Today, my God, what tortures of loneliness.
I wonder how long my heart will suffer this.
Tears rolled and rolled. Everyone sees my
weakness. My God give me courage . . .

Her room was furnished with only a pack-
ing-case which would serve as her desk, one
chair and some other wooden boxes which
would be put to use as seats. One other
person came with her, Charur Ma, who
had been the cook at St Mary's. The two
of them shopped for the supplies the bustee
school needed. Michael Gomez accompanied them whenever possible, begging for

medical supplies for the dispensary Sister Teresa was determined to establish.

14 Creek Lane quickly attracted those who wished to join Sister Teresa in her work. On 19 March 1949, Subashini Das, her former pupil and a boarder at St Mary's since she was nine, followed Sister Teresa's example, as she had predicted she might. She turned up at Creek Lane and asked if she could assist Sister Teresa in her work among the poor. Only a few weeks later, Magdalena Gomes, another old pupil, also joined them. Their number quickly swelled to ten within only a few months, although two decided to leave, having put their vocation to the test and found that they were not right for the work.

After a year, Sister Teresa's position had to be reviewed. Having taken Indian citizenship

during that year, Sister Teresa made it quite
clear that she had no intention of leaving. The
Archbishop of Calcutta saw that the best thing
to do would be to formalize the intentions
and rules for Sister Teresa's burgeoning new
community. He would apply to the office of
the Propagation of the Faith in Rome to have
the work of Sister Teresa and her followers
recognised as a congregation of his archdio-
cese. The first step was to draw up a constitu-
tion which would guide the Sisters. The new
congregation would be called the Missionaries of Charity and, in addition to the vows of
poverty, chastity and obedience, there would
be a fourth vow which would direct their
work: 'to give whole-hearted and free service
to the poorest of the poor.'

On 7 October 1950, a mass was held to
celebrate the inauguration of the new con-

gregation and Father van Exem read out the decree of recognition:

'To fulfil our mission of compassion and love, to the poorest of the poor we go – seeking out in towns and villages all over the world, even amid squalid surroundings, the poorest, the abandoned, the sick, the infirm, the leprosy patients, the dying, the desperate, the lost, the outcast, taking care of them, rendering help to them, visiting them assiduously, living Christ's love for them, and awakening their response to His great love.'

The founder of the Missionaries of Charity was also recognised with a new title: Sister Teresa was now Mother Teresa. Subashini Das would become Sister Agnes, and Magdalena Gomes became Sister Gertrude.

Within three years, the community had outgrown 14 Creek Lane and, in February 1953, the diocese bought 54a Lower Circular Road. Father van Exem used his contacts in the city and the property was bought from a Muslim family, who were moving to Dacca, at a price that barely covered the value of the land the house stood on. 54a Lower Circular Road thus became the Mother House of the Missionaries of Charity, where it remains to this day. The additional space meant that a chapel could be established, giving a new focus to the Sisters' work with the poor, sick, homeless and dying. From their new Mother House, the Sisters' difficult work continued.

Dressed in saris, the women sought out the poorest areas of Calcutta, where they found young children in desperate need of special care and where they tried to help anyone who was dying, whether in the gutters of busy streets or hidden away in alleyways. For Hindus, death involves elements of impurity and Hindu landlords disliked people dying in their accommodation. Likewise, rickshaw- and taxi-drivers might avoid taking seriously ill passengers. Worse still, hospitals were reluctant to admit patients they could do nothing for. The sight of the dead and the dying abandoned in the streets presented Mother Teresa with a clear priority. She must establish a home for the dying, some- where these people would always be ac- cepted and welcomed.

With a directness and humility that would characterise all her dealings with officialdom, Mother Teresa approached the Commis- sioner of Police and the Health Officer of

Calcutta and asked for their help in finding a
suitable place where the destitute might be
allowed to die with dignity. She was given a
simple pilgrims' hostel, Nirmal Hriday, near
the temple of Kalie in Kalighat. Kalighat is
still one of the most overcrowded parts of
south Calcutta and it is named after Kali, the
powerful Hindu goddess. Her ancient temple stands on the banks of a tributary to the
Ganges, sacred river of the Hindus. The
pilgrims' hostel was exactly what Mother
Teresa needed: it had gas, electricity and
there was lots of space, but it was filthy.
The Sisters' first job was to clean the entire
building and then they set about their real
task of giving a home to the dying.

While all holy people are treated with respect
in India, so much so that none of Mother
Teresa's followers ever encountered danger

from violence, some locals were unhappy about a Christian group working in such close proximity to a holy Hindu temple. Malicious rumours began to spread that the dying were being ministered the last rites and given Christian burials against their will. Dr Ahmad, the Chief Medical Officer, and a senior police official decided to visit Nirmal Hriday themselves. They saw Mother Teresa hunched over a figure whose face was little more than a terrible wound. Unobserved, they watched as Mother Teresa used tweezers to remove maggots from this wound, the smell of which would have been enough to keep most people from even entering the room. They heard Mother Teresa comforting the disfigured patient. She asked the patient to say a prayer to their god, while she would say one to hers.

Word had spread of the officials' visit to Nirmal Hriday and a crowd had gathered outside. The police officer told them that he would send Mother Teresa away only when they and their sisters and mothers came to do the work instead.

Despite the officials' clear support, tension in the local community continued. One day, a young temple priest was discovered to be dying of tuberculosis. There was no hope of a cure for him and the hospitals refused to give a bed to a hopeless case. He found himself in Nirmal Hriday, where Mother Teresa cared for him until he died. The other priests could not fail to notice the compassion she had shown, nor did they overlook the fact that Mother Teresa sent his body to be cremated according to the Hindu rites. Given this

Doing the washing at Nirmal Hriday

Calcutta street scene

example of her work, all resentment and
hostility faded away.

The Missionaries of Charity's declared aim is
to give the love they find in God to those
they care for and attend to. Many have
criticised Mother Teresa, believing that she
forces her own religious creed upon people
who are at their most vulnerable. Author and
feminist Germaine Greer wrote in the *Independent* on 22 September 1990: 'Mother
Teresa epitomized for me the blinkered
charitableness upon which we pride ourselves and for which we expect reward in
this world and the next.' Mother Teresa has
clearly stated, however, that neither she nor
any Missionary of Charity seeks converts.
Only those who request it are given a
Christian burial; to do otherwise would be
considered a sacrilege by the Missionaries of

Charity. Where medical science can do no more, Mother Teresa offers love and care to those who are abandoned by every member of their society, and ensures that they do not die alone.

The overwhelming impression of those who have sought to understand Mother Teresa is that her love of God motivates her every action. According to her faith, each body that she nurses is the body of Christ, and in loving those who come into her care she is loving Christ.

It was inevitable that Mother Teresa would identify another major group in Indian society who were abandoned and made outcasts through no fault of their own: lepers. No matter what their background, people with leprosy would leave their families so as not to bring disgrace to them or have them suffer in any way. While begging might be possible to begin with, the progress of the disease caused loss of feeling and susceptibility to further infection and loss of limb. Having tried and failed to set up a leprosy clinic when the only hospital to treat leprosy in the vast sprawl of Calcutta was closed after the uncharitable objections of locals and property developers, Mother Teresa could only turn to prayer.

One day, an ambulance was donated to the Missionaries and Mother Teresa saw that it could be transformed into a mobile clinic for leprosy. At the same time Dr Sen, a skin and leprosy specialist, offered his services to Mother Teresa for free. To Mother Teresa, it was the answer to her prayers. In September 1957, the first mobile leprosy

clinic was launched. Dr Sen treated the
lepers, but also trained the Sisters in this
specialized work. It was the first of many
clinics which would work by going to sites
where lepers were known to gather and then
returning a week later, treating the lepers and
keeping meticulous records. If patients went
missing one week, the Sisters would search
the area until they were found, to be sure
they were not in distress.

Mother Teresa also realised that she would
have to fight against the ignorance that
caused these people to be made outcasts.
She increased the awareness of the needs
of lepers, and groups began to appear col-
lecting donations to help the lepers. Not
only did people being to realise that lepers
could be helped, but the lepers themselves
began to feel that they were not being

Mother Teresa receives the Nobel Prize

A Sister feeds an orphan

abandoned altogether. Eventually, in 1969, the attitude towards lepers had changed so much that the government felt able to give an area of thirty-six acres to the Missionaries so that a town could be built as a home for the lepers. Mother Teresa called it Shanti Nagar, Town of Peace, because here the lepers could truly live in peace, without the fear of being moved on. They could also be offered treatment and, for those who could be cured, help was offered with rehabilitation so that they could return as full members of the wider community.

Children have always been of key importance to Mother Teresa as she has pursued her vocation. As the Missionaries of Charity grew and new convents were established, both in India and in other parts of the world, the Sisters also tried to open children's homes nearby, and these are called Shishu Bhawan. In these homes, the children may range in age from the tiniest infants to seven-year-olds and, apart from some of the younger children, they are educated at local schools. Any expenses, be it uniforms or books, are met by the Missionaries of Charity. Perhaps most well-known of all the many children's homes is Nirmala Shishu Bhavan, the Children's Home of the Immaculate, which is on Lower Circular Road, a short walk from the Mother House.

Many have reported how they have visited Nirmala Shishu Bhavan, expecting to find the atmosphere heavy with the children's feelings of abandonment. Here are children who have been plucked from pavements, out of rubbish-bins or from the arms of policemen who have found them on their doorsteps. There are also children from the Calcutta hospitals where Mother Teresa has told doctors that she will take any and all unwanted babies, saying, 'I'm fighting abortion with adoption.' Many of the children are sick and some of them are terminally ill, but in Nirmala Shishu Bhavan all of them are cared for and loved by the Sisters.

Mother Teresa has tried particularly hard to establish Shishu Bhawans at each of the leprosy centres so that parents with leprosy can pass their children into the care of the Sisters. Parents are still able to visit their children, but are discouraged from touching or kissing them as this exposes them to the risk of infection.

Over the years, the Missionaries of Charity have spread all over the world to form a network of schools, dispensaries, homes for abandoned children and for leprosy sufferers, for alcoholics and for drug addicts, for the destitute and the dying. More recently, they have also established centres for those with AIDS. Today, there are some 500 Missionaries of Charity centres around the world. For the first ten years, and in accordance with the regulations of the Roman Catholic Church, the Missionaries of Charity did not take their work beyond Calcutta. Mother Teresa was reportedly impatient with this restriction, but the Archbishop of Calcutta, ever-cautious, would not bend the rules for her.

In 1960 she was allowed to open her first centre outside Calcutta, which she promptly did in a town called Ranchi. The next was in Delhi and Prime Minister Jawaharlal Nehru opened it even though he was unwell at the time. When Mother Teresa asked him if she could tell him about the work of the Missionaries, he answered, 'No, Mother, you do no need to tell me about your work. I already know about it, that is why I am here.' In 1962 she was the first person who was not Indian by birth to receive the prestigious Padma Shri award from the President of India. Nehru had commended her for it.

Once it was made possible, expansion was rapid. Twenty-five centres were open in India by the end of the 1960s, eighty-six by the end of the 1980s, and now there are nearly two hundred. The first house to be opened outside India was in Venezuela in 1965. It was the Papal Nuncio in New Delhi, Archbishop Knox, who thought that

the Missionaries of Charity were needed in
Venezuela. While the Archbishop of Calcutta had been reluctant to let Mother
Teresa's community grow too rapidly, he
could not stand in the way of the Papal
Nuncio. It is interesting to note that in
February 1965 the Missionaries of Charity
became a congregation of pontifical right,
which meant that they were no longer
answerable to the Archbishop of Calcutta,
but to the Vatican. Mother Teresa was
invited by the Bishop of Venezuela to assess
the situation herself and this became the
pattern for the opening of all new centres:
the local bishop would invite Mother Teresa
and she would visit the country herself. She
was going to be very busy.

In 1968 the second overseas house was
opened in Rome; in 1969 two were estab-

Sisters feed the sick at Nirmal Hriday

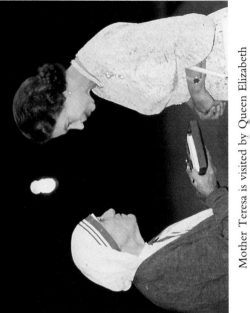

Mother Teresa is visited by Queen Elizabeth

lished in Australia. 1970 added four more, one each in London and Jordan, and another two in Venezuela. Then came New York, Bangladesh, Northern Ireland, the Gaza Strip, Yemen, Ethiopia, Sicily, Papua New Guinea, the Philippines, Panama, Japan, Portugal, Brazil and Burundi. More houses have opened in Britain and America, and they can now be found in what was once the Soviet Union, in South Africa and all over Eastern Europe, including Albania, Mother Teresa's home country.

At each of these centres, the work has been carried out by an ever-expanding number of missionaries. Naturally, many have wished to test their vocation and training-centres for noviciates have sprung up alongside work-centres. Men have also been inspired to join Mother Teresa and

1963 saw the founding of the Missionaries of Charity Brothers.

In 1961, Mother Teresa had called on Father van Exem to ask for his help with a particular matter. It had become obvious that the help of some men might be useful in the supervision of the older boys and with some of the heavier work. She asked Father van Exem if he could help her to find some suitable candidates. In due course, some Brothers were sent to Calcutta and were housed at Shishu Bhawan, but it became apparent that the Brothers needed a different environment. More critically, some were reluctant to join because the Brothers were not officially recognised by the Roman Catholic Church. The spiritual guidance of the Brothers was being shared between Father Henry and Mother Teresa, but this was unsatisfactory in the long term because the Roman Catholic Church does not allow women to head male communities.

Mother Teresa began to search for a priest who would lead the Brothers. Father Ian Travers-Ball, a Jesuit priest, arrived in Shishu Bhavan, where he knew Mother Teresa was guiding a group of young men, intending to stay a month or so to learn what he could. A tall, charismatic and articulate man, he had arrived in India from Australia in 1954 and become interested in the poor whilst working in the mining district of Hazaribagh. Finding that the work being done at Shishu Bhavan moved him deeply and realising that the community was in need of a priest, Father Travers-Ball accepted Mother Teresa's invitation to stay on as the Brothers' priest when his month ended. The arrangement was provisional, as he had to seek the permission of his Jesuit superiors in order to take up the position. At last a letter arrived from the Society of Jesus in Rome in January 1966, granting him three options. He chose the third, which meant leaving the Society of Jesus (as Mother Teresa had left the Sisters of Loreto) and joining the Missionaries of Charity Brothers. He chose the title of General Servant for his new role as head of the male congregation, and took the religious name of Father Andrew.

Over the years, the work of the Brothers has developed in subtly different ways from that of the Sisters, although it is all done in the same spirit. The Brothers are less regimented and enclosed than the women, and have needed to adapt themselves more closely to the varied cultures in which they have found themselves working. The first overseas house the Brothers established was in war-ravaged Vietnam in the 1970s, where the Sisters did not have a presence. This has become the pattern they have worked to. In cities and countries where the Sisters have not yet established themselves, the Brothers have set to work. In Los Angeles, Hong Kong, Japan, Taiwan, Korea, Guatemala, the Philippines, El Salvador, the Dominican Republic, Brazil and Madagascar, they have taken up the tasks they could best perform: establishing shelters for homeless boys, alcoholics and drug addicts.

It may seem that whatever Mother Teresa needed to continue her work would eventually present itself. On the other hand, she has also known how to absorb every available offer of help and been able to put those offers to the best possible use. In 1954, the wife of a British business man working in India, Ann Blaikie, offered to make toys that Christmas for the children in Mother Teresa's care. Toys were not needed as badly as clothes and Mother Teresa asked Ann to turn her skills to this end instead.

She took Ann to Nirmal Hriday, the Home for the Dying in Kalighat, and by the end of the day Ann Blaikie had changed from a well-meaning housewife to the woman who would establish the first Co-Workers group in Calcutta. She gathered a group of women together to make the clothes that were needed for that Christmas. They were duly thanked by Mother Teresa, who then pointed out to them that the two big festivals of the Hindu and Muslim calenders were fast approaching and that the other

Early morning mass at Nirmal Hriday

Pope John Paul II visits Calcutta

children were now looking forward to their new clothes as well. The work would have to go on.

When she returned to Britain, Ann discovered others who had come into contact with Mother Teresa and wanted to continue to help her and the Co-Workers spread to Britain as well. Wherever a new centre has opened, Co-Workers would appear too. Though their exact numbers are unknown, it is estimated that Britain has more than 30,000 and the United States some 10,000, which gives an indication of the size of this vast network of helpers.

The woman who started her mission with only five rupees to her name has never involved herself or her fellow Sisters in fund-raising as such. When she first began

her work in Motijhil bustee, she would visit
the local priests and beg for donations which
would allow her to continue her work –
some were generous, while others were
critical and unhelpful. These men might be
forgiven for their mixed reactions to her
pleas, for this European woman in the
cheapest kind of sari, with a small cloth
bag slung over her shoulder and sturdy
sandals on her feet was hardly conven-
tional, she did not even look like a nun
anymore. Mendicancy is part of India's
ancient traditions, so while she met with
some resistance at first, many were unflinch-
ing in their support. She has continued to
work in the complete faith that God will
provide whatever is needed, and even more
deep-seated is her belief that she does not
really need anything to answer God's call.
On the other hand, just as she has never

turned away those who wished to help, she has never refused a gift which could be made to serve the Missionaries' work. When Pope Paul VI visited Bombay in 1965, he gave Mother Teresa a white Cadillac which had been a gift to him. Unlike the old ambulance which became her first mobile leprosy clinic, Mother Teresa could find no practical use for the ostentatious car. So she raffled it and raised some money which was of use in her work.

In much the same spirit, she has avoided all attempts to glorify her role in the work of the Missionaries. When people have asked her about her past and about the early influences on her life, she has always been reticent and has only become animated when the conversation has turned to the work of her community. For many, though, Mother

Teresa, her face now lined with the many creases of age and years of care, is inseparable from any of the work of the Missionaries.

The most striking illustration of this is that despite Mother Teresa's own wish to resign as Superior of her Order, her followers have persistently refused to let her step down. Even after she had been seriously ill and had sought permission to convene a special General Chapter in September 1990 so that a successor could be appointed, her Sisters voted unanimously to retain her as their Superior.

There can be no doubt that her work has had a profound effect on many people around the world, even on those in the highest positions of society and government. In 1980, for example, Prince Charles made a

A small child finds comfort

LET EVERY ACTION OF MINE BE SOMETHING BEAUTIFUL FOR GOD

MOTHER 1948

Mother Teresa's motto

special journey to visit her mission in Calcutta during his tour of India. He would have met her again with Princess Diana in 1992, except that she was in poor health. When Princess Diana returned to Britain, she went to Rome where Mother Teresa was convalescing. The two women, who lead such different lives, spent some time together in conversation and prayer. Mother Teresa did not just wait to be visited when Pope John Paul II asked her to be his envoy to Lebanon in 1982; she rescued thirty-seven mentally handicapped children from a hospital which had been bombed in the war. Mother Teresa has also been forthright in her criticism: she drew the attention of the British Prime Minister, Margaret Thatcher, to Britain's acute housing problems. When the Gulf War began, she pleaded with President Bush and President Saddam Hus-

sein to end the hostilities before many
innocent lives were wrecked. As soon as
the war was over, she got the Iraqi President's permission to open half a dozen
centres in the war-torn country so that she
could begin to put right the damage they had
done.

Many countries and organisations have recognised her work by awarding her their
most prestigious prizes. The one which
captured every headline around the world
was the Nobel Peace Prize, which she
received in 1979. Her humility on such
occasions has been complete, and the
money which has so often accompanied
them has all contributed to the work of
the Missionaries. Mother Teresa continues
to fulfil her own part in that work, which
means that she has often spent as much as half

the year travelling to visit centres around the world. Finding herself consulted on the particular problems at a centre, she will try to offer advice and help in solving them. Then there are the invitations to give talks, to visit the sick, to inspect sites for new centres, as well as the constant stream of visitors, both grand and ordinary, who seek her help with complicated issues, or simply ask for her blessing. Her business card, which she gives to anyone who will take it, reads:

> The fruit of Silence is Prayer
> The fruit of Prayer is Faith
> The fruit of Faith is Love
> The fruit of Love is Service
> The fruit of Service is Peace.

Leaving the other Sisters to retire to bed at 10 p.m., Mother Teresa then attends to her correspondence and other administrative demands. She has often worked into the small hours. A diminutive woman of extraordinary strength, Mother Teresa remains the most powerful exemplar of the mission she set out on eighty-four years ago: to serve the poorest of the poor.

A Calcutta street in 1930

CHRONOLOGY

1910

August, Agnes Bojaxhui is born on 26 August, youngest of Nikola and Drana's three children to be brought up in Skopje.

1918

Agnes's father dies suddenly.

1924

Lazar, Agnes' brother, leaves home to join a military academy in Austria.

1925

Father Jambrenkoic becomes the local pastor. Agnes joins the Sodality of the Blessed Virgin Mary set up by the pastor.

1928

Agnes, together with her mother and sister, make their last trip to Letnice together. It is here that she realises the time has come for her to follow her vocation.

September, Agnes is accepted by the Order of Loreto Nuns.

1929

January, Agnes arrives in Calcutta, moving on to Darjeeling where she is to complete her training as a novice.

1931

May Agnes takes her first vows as a sister, becoming Sister Teresa.

1937

May, Sister Teresa takes her lifelong vows. She then moves on to Entally, an eastern district of Calcutta.

1946

September; Sister Teresa receives a message from God, to renounce her life at the convent and go to the slums to work and live among the poor.

1948

August, the letter from Rome finally arrives allowing Sister Teresa to leave the Loreto Order but remain a nun. Sister Teresa sets out for Petna, where the Sisters of the Medical Mission introduce her to some basic medical skills. After four months she returns to Calcutta to the house of The Little Sisters of the Poor.

1949

February, Sister Teresa moves to 14 Creek Lane. In March she is joined by Subashini Das, her former pupil, soon to be joined by other former pupils. Later becomes an Indian citizen.

1950

October, a mass to celebrate the inauguration of the new congregation, the Missionaries of Charities, is held.

1953

February, additional space is needed so 54a Lower Circular Road becomes the Mother House of the

Mission of Charities. Sister Teresa is now Mother Teresa, she continues her work with the sick and dying. Mother Teresa approaches the Commissioner of Police and the Health Officer of Calcutta and manages to secure a simple pilgrims' hostel, which is to become Nirmal Hriday.

1957
September, the first mobile leprosy clinic is launched.

1960
The first Missionary of Charity opens outside Calcutta in Ranchi.

1962
Mother Teresa is the first person who was not Indian by birth to receive the prestigious Padma Shri.

1963
The Missionaries of Charity Brothers is founded.

1965

The first house outside India is opened in Venezuela. Pope Paul the VI visits Bombay, he presents Mother Teresa with a white Cadillac, which she raffles to raise money.

1969

The government gives an area of thirty-six acres to the Missionaries so that a home for the lepers can be built. By the end of the 60s, twenty-five centres have been opened.

1979

Mother Teresa is awarded the Nobel Peace Prize.

1980

Prince Charles makes a special journey to visit the Mission in Calcutta.

1990

Despite her wish to step down, the Sisters vote unanimously to retain Mother Teresa as their Superior.

1992

Princess Diana goes to Rome to visit Mother Teresa who is convalescing.

Over the years the Missionaries of Charity have spread all over the world. Today there are some 500 Missionaries of Charity. Mother Teresa continues her work throughout the Calcutta centre, serving the poorest of the poor.

LIFE AND TIMES

Julius Caesar
Hitler
Monet
Van Gogh
Beethoven
Mozart
Mother Teresa
Florence Nightingale
Anne Frank
Napoleon

LIFE AND TIMES

JFK
Martin Luther King
Marco Polo
Christopher Columbus
Stalin
William Shakespeare
Oscar Wilde
Castro
Gandhi
Einstein

FURTHER MINI SERIES INCLUDE

ILLUSTRATED POETS

Robert Burns
Shakespeare
Oscar Wilde
Emily Dickinson
Christina Rossetti
Shakespeare's Love Sonnets

FURTHER MINI SERIES
INCLUDE

HEROES OF THE WILD WEST

General Custer
Butch Cassidy and the Sundance Kid
Billy the Kid
Annie Oakley
Buffalo Bill
Geronimo
Wyatt Earp
Doc Holliday
Sitting Bull
Jesse James

FURTHER MINI SERIES
INCLUDE

THEY DIED TOO YOUNG

Elvis
James Dean
Buddy Holly
Jimi Hendrix
Sid Vicious
Marc Bolan
Ayrton Senna
Marilyn Monroe
Jim Morrison

THEY DIED TOO YOUNG

Malcolm X
Kurt Cobain
River Phoenix
John Lennon
Glenn Miller
Isadora Duncan
Rudolph Valentino
Freddie Mercury
Bob Marley